Play
Ball

Play Ball

BASEBALL FUN, FACTS, AND TRIVIA

BARBOUR
PUBLISHING, INC.
Uhrichsville, Ohio

ISBN 1-57748-429-0

Published by Barbour Publishing, Inc., P.O. Box 719, Uhrichsville, OH 44683 http://www.barbourbooks.com

Member of the
Evangelical Christian
Publishers Association

Printed in the United States of America.

Introduction

The Perfect Ballplayer

Why certainly I'd like to have that fellow who hits a home run every time at bat, who strikes out every opposing batter when he's pitching, who throws strikes to any base or the plate when he's playing outfield, and who's always thinking about two innings ahead just what he'll do to baffle the other team. Any manager would want a guy like that playing for him. The only trouble is to get him to put down his [drink] and come down out of the stands and do those things.

—MANAGER DANNY MURTAUGH

Perfection is rarely achieved in any field of endeavor. Such is the case with baseball.

The very best hitters, those with batting averages over .300, fail to reach base safely more than sixty percent of the time. The most dominating pitchers, those with an earned run average around two, are still allowing the opposition to score. And when is the last time you heard of a starter going undefeated for a season?

Actually, in baseball, it's the imperfections that make each game a contest. If we expected hitters to slug home runs every time at bat, where would the drama be? And if every pitcher threw a perfect game each time out, things would become monotonous quickly. Fortunately, that's not the case.

Baseball is a wonderfully enjoyable game, a deeply American tradition with a worldwide following. In many ways, it mirrors life itself with its twists and turns, and moments both dull and dramatic. Read on for some of the history, humor, and highlights of the game. Meet some of the stars, the characters, and a few players who have found one way to achieve "perfection"—spiritual perfection, that is, through faith in Jesus Christ. Their stories are told by the writers of *Sports Spectrum* magazine.

From baseball's creation in 1839, to Mark McGwire and Sammy Sosa's memorable home run chase in 1998, this book highlights many of the most interesting tidbits you'll ever find on the game you love. Are you ready to begin? *Play Ball!*

from **SPORTS** spectrum

Tony Fernandez

I Need Something Better in My Life

Tony Fernandez made his major league debut on September 2, 1983. He holds the American League career record for highest fielding percentage by a shortstop (1,000 or more games) at .982; holds the American League record for most games played in a season by a shortstop (163 in 1986); was named to *The Sporting News* All-Star team in 1987; captured Gold Glove at shortstop in 1986, 1987, 1988, and 1989; led the American League in triples in 1990 (17); led National League third basemen in fielding percentage in 1994 (.991); holds the record for triples by a Toronto Blue Jay; and is a seasoned veteran of both All-Star and World Series games.

"I reached my childhood dream when I was called up to the big leagues," Tony says. But the fulfillment of his dream did not bring satisfaction. "There was nothing there. God had made me a ballplayer as I had asked Him to earlier. When I reached that level and found I was still empty, I asked, 'What's going on? This is not what I thought it would be.' I was happy to make it to the majors, but it was not what I was looking for. There was still something missing. At that point I realized I needed something bigger.

"I thank God for my parents and what they did and what they taught me early in my life. I always had a respect for God. I had a great foundation for my life, but it wasn't until 1984, after I broke my wrist, that I understood how to have a personal relationship with Him. People always talk about religion, but I found out that religion is man-made. What God wants is a relationship.

"Jesse Barfield and Roy Lee Jackson were on the team at the time, and I remember Jesse telling me, 'You know, Jesus loves you and He wants to bless you more than He already has.' And I said, 'I know—I grew up in a Christian home.' I thought having Christian parents was an automatic ticket to heaven.

"Jesse kept witnessing to me, but I thought I knew all about God. I went down to Triple A for a month for a rehab program after spring training. The Blue Jays called me back up after about five weeks, but I wasn't playing much. I was disappointed."

Soon, though, Fernandez would begin to discover the answer. It began with one play. His life, like many good baseball games, turned on one play. "We were playing in Boston on June 24, 1984. It was a Saturday game, and I made a beautiful play in the hole. Everyone was commenting on the play, but the manager didn't say anything good—something I would like to hear; some approval or some encouragement. I was a rookie. I wanted to hear something positive. When asked [about the play] by the media, the manager just said [the play] was routine. He was used to it. I guess I was looking for glory."

PLAY BALL

After reading the write-up in the Sunday paper the next day, Tony discussed the situation with a childhood friend from the Dominican Republic. He told him, "I need something better in my life."

That day, after the baseball chapel service, Fernandez decided it was time to give his life to Jesus. "I remember walking out of the chapel, across the locker room, and I called to Jesse. I said, 'Jesse, hey, I think I'm ready to accept Christ.' He said, 'Do you think you're really ready?' Then he looked me straight in the eyes and said, 'I think you are,' and he called Roy Lee Jackson and the other ones [from the chapel service]. I remember that right at that moment I gave my life to Jesus.

"Ever since, I have been trying to please God in every way in my work," says Fernandez.

You can't sit on a lead and run a few plays into the line and just kill the clock. You've got to throw the ball over the plate and give the other man his chance. That's why baseball is the greatest game of them all.

EARL WEAVER,
Former Baltimore manager

Errors are part of my image. One night in Pittsburgh, thirty thousand fans gave me a standing ovation when I caught a hot dog wrapper on the fly.

DICK "STONEFINGERS" STUART,
First baseman for the Phillies, Pirates, Mets, Dodgers, Angels and Red Sox in the sixties

In the Beginning

The Origin of Baseball

The Mills Commission was appointed in 1905 to determine the origin of baseball. The committee's formation was urged by Albert G. Spalding, one of the game's pioneers, following an article by Henry Chadwick, a famous early baseball writer, who contended that the sport evolved from the English game of rounders.

During its three-year study, the committee was deluged with communications on the subject. The testimony of Abner Graves, a mining engineer from Denver, Colorado, in support of Abner Doubleday figured prominently in the committee's inquiry.

Graves and Doubleday had attended school together in Cooperstown, New York. Doubleday later was appointed to the U.S. Military Academy at West Point, graduating in 1842. As a captain, he fired the first gun for the Union at Fort Sumter, South Carolina.

In letters to Spalding, Graves claimed to have been present when Doubleday made changes to the then popular game of "Town Ball," which involved twenty to fifty boys in a field attempting to catch a ball hit by a "tosser" using a four-inch flat bat. According to Graves, Doubleday used a stick to mark out a diamond-shaped field in the dirt. His other refinements ostensibly included limiting the number of players, adding bases (hence the name, "baseball") and the concept of a pitcher and catcher.

The committee's final report in 1907 stated in part that "the first scheme for playing baseball, according to the best evidence obtainable to date, was devised by Abner Doubleday at Cooperstown, N.Y. in 1839."

PLAY BALL

The Beginning of
Professional Baseball

Baseball's first recorded match was played at the Elysian Fields in Hoboken, New Jersey, on June 19, 1846. The New York Nine lost to Alexander Cartwright's New York Knickerbockers, 23–1.

In 1858, the National Association of Baseball Players was organized, making the rules of the sport more uniform. Baseball's popularity grew throughout the 1850s and 1860s. The sport was even played by soldiers during the Civil War.

The Cincinnati Red Stockings of 1869, organized by Harry Wright, a jeweler and former star cricket player, was baseball's first all-professional team. During the 1869 season the Red Stockings traveled 12,000 miles and played baseball throughout the Northeast and West. The team won sixty-four games and there was one disputed tie. The following season the Cincinnati streak reached ninety-two straight wins. The fabled success of the Red Stockings ended the days of amateur-only competition and triggered the beginnings of professional baseball.

You look forward to it like a birthday party when you're a kid. You think something wonderful is going to happen.
Yankee Great JOE DIMAGGIO,
on Opening Day

Every member of our baseball team at West Point became a general: This proves the value of team sports.
GENERAL OMAR BRADLEY

PLAY BALL

The Baseball Shrine of Pigtown

In 1909, a man named Charles Hercules Ebbets began secretly buying up adjacent parcels of land in the Flatbush section of Brooklyn, including the site of a garbage dump called Pigtown because of the pigs that once ate their fill there and the stench that still filled the air. He hoped eventually to build a permanent home for the lackluster baseball team he had once worked for and now owned. The team was called the Trolley Dodgers, or just the Dodgers, after the way their devoted fans negotiated Brooklyn's busy streets.

In 1912, construction began. By the time it was completed a year later, Pigtown had been transformed into Ebbets Field—baseball's newest shrine, where some of the game's greatest drama would take place. In 1955, after more than four decades of frustration, Brooklyn would finally win a world championship, only to know, two years later, the ultimate heartbreak, as their team moved to a new city three thousand miles away, leaving an empty shell in Flatbush that eventually became an apartment building, and an even emptier spot in the soul of every Brooklyn fan.

I'm not an athlete. I'm a professional baseball player.
Former Phillie JOHN KRUK

This is a tough park for a hitter when the air conditioning is blowing in.

Catcher BOB BOONE,
on the Astrodome in Houston

PLAY BALL

The House Built for Ruth

Yankee Stadium was shaped like a horseshoe with three tiers of grandstand stretching in foul territory from the left field line around behind home plate out to the right field line. Rows and rows of wooden bleachers sat behind the outfield. Because the stadium was designed to take advantage of the left-handed power of Babe Ruth, the architect made it easier to hit home runs to right field and right center than to left and left center, thus removing all symmetry but at the same time giving the stadium its unique dimensions. Down the lines home runs were easy if a pitcher was foolish enough to allow the batter to pull the ball. It was 296 feet in right and 301 in left, and from both foul lines the stands dropped back deeply toward straightaway center field, and hitting home runs into the power alleys, 407 feet from the plate over a fourteen-foot wall in right and 457 feet over a thirteen-foot wall in left, took strength of a Ruthian nature. Dead center was 461 feet, Death Valley because 425-foot towering blasts became routine outs, ruining many batting averages.

Ideally, the umpire should combine the integrity of a Supreme Court judge, the physical agility of an acrobat, the endurance of Job and the imperturbability of Buddha.
Time Magazine, 8/25/61

Trying to sneak a fastball past Hank Aaron is like trying to sneak the sunrise past a rooster.
Milwaukee Brave JOE ADCOCK

from **SPORTS spectrum**

Andy
Benes

The Benes Factor

In 1989 Andy Benes split his year among Wichita (Texas
League), Las Vegas (Pacific Coast League), and San
Diego (National League). He was named Texas League
Pitcher of the Year and National League Rookie Pitcher of
the Year; got his first major league home run on
September 3, 1989 off Dennis Cook (career batting average: .139 with four home runs); captured two 1-0 victories
over Orel Hershiser in 1989; career record entering 1998
season: 104-94 with a 3.64 ERA and 1,416 strikeouts in
1,705 innings. Benes put together a 10-game winning
streak in 1991; pitched in the 1993 All-Star Game; and
won the 1994 National League strikeout title (189).

Andy Benes is the ace of the Arizona Diamondbacks' pitching staff. Although he's a nine-year veteran
pitching for an expansion ball club, Benes is the same
no-nonsense workhorse he's always been. He'll com-
pete every fifth day and give his team at least seven
strong innings per start. And perhaps more important,
he's still legitimately concerned about helping people in

his community—particularly children.

It may seem easy for a millionaire ballplayer like Benes to throw some money at a charitable cause, get some good publicity, and never really dig in. But that's not Andy Benes. He digs in when helping others like he does on the mound while clinging to a one-run lead in the ninth. He's more interested in helping the cause, and helping others, than he is in receiving personal glory.

Few would have known of his trip to Costa Rica had it not been the place where he agreed to terms with Arizona. Yet Andy was there helping others.

Ex-big leaguer Don Gordon, of the baseball ministry Unlimited Potential, Inc., says Andy's desire to reach out is pure. "He's off the charts as far as community involvement. He's community-minded, but not for personal gain. Andy does it out of the goodness of his heart."

That's why Benes, despite pitching for his fourth team in four years, continues his involvement with a campaign called "Strikeouts for Kids." He started working with the program while in San Diego. Every time he strikes out a batter, the bank account of Children's Ministries International (CMI) gets one hundred dollars richer.

CMI is a ministry that seeks to introduce the love of Christ to grade school age children at weekend retreats across the country. "Andy and Jennifer have a heart for God, a heart for kids, and a heart for helping others," says Steve Karges, president of CMI. "They have really provided a boost to our ministry."

Benes reaches out to ministries such as CMI and in countries such as Costa Rica because he has a passion for helping others know the truth he has found in a personal relationship with Jesus Christ.

"I grew up in church," says Andy. "I knew a lot of

Bible verses and went to church every Sunday. Although I knew a lot about Christianity and I had a belief in Jesus Christ, I hadn't asked Him to be my Savior. I did that in August of 1989 at a baseball chapel meeting in Montreal.

"I have a wonderful wife, four healthy children, and a wonderful job that pays well. But at some point, all of those things are going to let you down. The one thing that can be constant in your life is your faith. Jesus says He will never leave us or forsake us (Hebrews 13:5). Regardless of what church you go to, you have to know Jesus Christ and know Him as your Savior!"

While Benes may be one of baseball's top starting pitchers, he isn't arrogant and doesn't get caught up with himself. Former Cardinal teammate Danny Sheaffer says, "He really has a focus on his relationship with Christ and with his wife, and not letting the game take control of him."

Andy clearly sees the much bigger picture. "I love what I'm doing. But just to be able to play baseball, that's not important," explains Benes. "In the whole scheme of things, we're entertainers. I look at it [baseball] as an opportunity to reach people."

That's the Benes factor that has made this high-profile pitcher a benefactor to more and more people each day.

When you're in a slump, it's almost as if you look out at the field and it's one big glove.

Utility infielder VANCE LAW

There have been only two geniuses in the world: Willie Mays and Willie Shakespeare.

TALLULAH BANKHEAD,
Actress (1903-1968)

Highlights

The Modern World Series Begins

A. G. Spalding, President
Chicago League Club
Chicago

Dear Sir,

The championship season is fast approaching an end, and it now seems reasonably sure that the Chicago White Stockings and St. Louis Brown Stockings will win the championship of their respective associations. I therefore take this opportunity of challenging your team on behalf of the Browns, for a series of contests to be known as the World's Championship Series. It is immaterial to me whether the series be composed of five, seven, or nine games. I would respectfully suggest, however, that it would be better for a financial standpoint to play the entire series on the two home grounds, and not to travel around as we did last season. I would like to hear from you at your earliest convenience, in order that the dates and other details may be arranged. I am yours respectfully,

C. Von Der Ahe
St. Louis
September 26, 1886

When you go through a game, make every pitch like it was the last pitch that you'll ever call—you'll have a good game!

EDWIN D. MERRILL,
American League Umpire

PLAY BALL

World Series Appearances (through 1998 season)

Team	Wins	Losses	Last Appearance	Last Championship
Yankees	24	11	1998	1998
Cardinals	9	6	1987	1982
Athletics	9	5	1990	1989
Dodgers	6	12	1988	1988
Giants	5	11	1989	1954
Reds	5	4	1990	1990
Red Sox	5	4	1986	1918
Pirates	5	2	1979	1979
Tigers	4	5	1984	1984
Braves	3	5	1996	1995
Orioles	3	4	1983	1983
Cubs	2	8	1945	1908
Blue Jays	2	0	1993	1993
Indians	2	3	1997	1948
White Sox	2	2	1959	1917
Twins	2	1	1991	1991
Mets	2	1	1986	1986
Phillies	1	4	1993	1980
Royals	1	1	1985	1985
Marlins	1	0	1997	1997
Padres	0	2	1998	—
Brewers	0	1	1982	—

Teams with no World Series appearances through 1998 season: Angels, Astros, Expos, Mariners, Rangers, Rockies, Diamondbacks, Devil Rays.

PLAY BALL

Red Sox Win the Series!

On October 15, 1923, the Yankees beat the Giants, 6-4, to win their first World Series. The pinstriped champions included former Red Sox "Jumping Joe" Dugan, Wally Schang, Everett Scott, "Bullet Joe" Bush, Herb Pennock, Waite Hoyt, and Babe Ruth.

The next day's Boston *Herald* ran a team photo of the World Series winners with the bitter headline: "Red Sox Alumni Become Champions of the Baseball World."

People ask me what I do in winter when there's no baseball. I'll tell you what I do. I stare out the window and wait for spring.

Hall of Famer ROGERS HORNSBY

Kids today are looking for idols, but sometimes they look too far....They don't have to look any farther than their home because those are the people that love you. They are the real heroes.

Dodger third baseman BOBBY BONILLA

I believe in the Rip Van Winkle Theory: that a man from 1910 must be able to wake up after being asleep for seventy years, walk into a ballpark and understand baseball perfectly.

BOWIE KUHN,
Commissioner of Baseball (1969-1984)

PLAY BALL

The National League and Jackie Robinson

The biggest sports story of 1947 was a two-sentence announcement by the Brooklyn Dodgers on April 10: "Brooklyn announces the purchase of the contract of Jack Roosevelt Robinson from Montreal. He will report immediately."

Stanley Woodward of the New York *Herald-Tribune* wrote that the [St. Louis] Cardinals had planned a protest strike when the Dodgers came to St. Louis and were in fact trying to foment a strike by all the teams in the National League because of Brooklyn's black player [Jackie Robinson]. League President Ford Frick sent this message to the Cardinals:

"If you do this you will be suspended from the league. You will find that the friends you think you have in the press box will not support you, that you will be outcasts. I do not care if half the league strikes. Those who do it will encounter quick retribution. They will be suspended, and I don't care if it wrecks the National League for five years. This is the United States of America, and one citizen has as much right to play as another. The National League will go down the line with Robinson whatever the consequence."

I think a baseball field must be the most beautiful thing in the world. It's so honest and precise. And we play on it. Every star gets humbled. Every mediocre player has a great moment.

LOWELL COHN in *The Temple of Baseball* (1981)

PLAY BALL

Baseball is not life itself. . .

. . .although the resemblance keeps coming up. It's probably a good idea to keep the two sorted out, but old fans, if they are anything like me, can't help noticing how cunningly our game replicates the larger schedule, with its beguiling April optimism; the cheerful roughhouse of June; the grinding, serious, unending (surely) business of midsummer; the September settling of accounts, when hopes must be traded in for philosophies or brave smiles; and then the abrupt running-down of autumn, when we wish for—almost demand—a prolonged and glittering final adventure just before the curtain. But nowhere is this metaphor more insistent than in baseball's sense of slippage; our rueful, fleeting awareness that we tend to pay attention to the wrong things—to last night's rally and tomorrow's pitching match-up—while lesser and sweeter moments slide by unperceived. Players notice this too. Bob Gibson, the most competitive man I have ever seen on a ball field, once told me that what he missed most after he had retired wasn't the competition at all. "I don't miss the pitching but I can't say I don't miss the game," the Cardinal Hall of Famer said. "I miss it a *little*. There's a lot I don't want to get back to. . . . I think it's the life I miss—all the activity that's around baseball. I don't miss playing baseball but I miss. . .baseball. *Baseball.* Does that sound like a crazy man?"

I am the most loyal player money can buy.

DON SUTTON,
Pitcher for the Los Angeles
Dodgers, Houston Astros, Milwaukee Brewers,
Oakland Athletics and California Angels

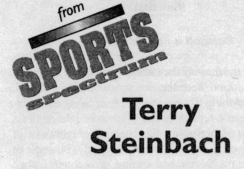

from

SPORTS
spectrum

Terry
Steinbach

Catching the Rock

That Minnesota Twins catcher Terry Steinbach chose to move to the Twin Cities before the 1997 season tells a lot about him. While one of the reasons he left the Oakland Athletics after eleven years as a mainstay by the bay was to be closer to his parents and his wife's parents, the New Ulm, Minnesota native also transferred to the Metrodome so he could play for Tom Kelly.

It would be easy for a baseball player who's a Christian to be a bit wary of signing on with Kelly. Since the controversy a decade or so ago when Gary Gaetti became a Christian and took some heat about it from the Twins' leadership, believers in Jesus haven't exactly been welcomed with open arms.

For Steinbach, the challenge of playing for Kelly outweighed possible negative factors. Steinbach says, "We had some great battles [with the Twins]. I've been on the other side, with Oakland and Minnesota challenging each other. T.K. has been around a long time, and it was important to play for a quality manager."

Besides, Steinbach feels that the previous controversy

about Christian players is "getting put aside." One reason for that, he says, is the excellence of some of today's Christian players and the way they are not afraid to be aggressive on the field. "John Wetteland was a great example of that a couple of years ago. And Aggie [Rick Aguilera of the Twins] fits that category." So does Steinbach.

To illustrate his point, Steinbach tells of a chapel message he heard when he was with the A's. "It was at the World Series with the Giants, and the chapel speaker talked about David and Goliath. He told us that not only did David kill the giant, but he cut his head off. Now what kind of a wimp is that? He was saying, 'If you happen to be a Christian athlete, you don't have to be passive or timid.' "

Steinbach is neither, yet he knows he can't go it alone. "The great thing to me," he says, "is that if you're sound in the Lord, there's always a place to go when things go wrong."

No matter where Steinbach plays, he knows that the place to go is Jesus, the One the catcher calls "the Solid Rock."

Umpire's Heaven is a place where he works third base every game. Home is where the heartache is.
                                        Umpire RON LUCIANO

I knew it would ruin my arm, but one year of 25-7 is worth five of 15-15.
                                Former Oriole pitcher STEVE STONE

The Art of Hitting
Cobb's Average at Fifty-two

Ty Cobb was a proud, fiercely competitive man whose volcanic emotions lay just beneath the surface, ready to erupt at the slightest tremor. One of the tremors that constantly ignited Cobb was any questioning of his abilities, especially when his talents were compared to those of later-day players. And so it was that when Cobb appeared at the 1939 World's Fair in Flushing Meadows and a reporter asked him how he'd do against modern pitching. Cobb, without batting the proverbial lash, answered, "I'd probably hit about .320, maybe .325." The reporter swallowed hard and asked the next obvious question: "But Mr. Cobb, your lifetime average was .367 and you've always said you felt the pitchers of today weren't as good as those you faced. Why," he went on, "do you think you'd only hit .320 now?"

"You've got to remember something, sonny," the irascible Cobb snapped. "I'm fifty-two years old now!"

They can holler at the uniform all they want, but when they holler at the man wearing the uniform, they're in trouble.

Umpire JOE BRINKMAN

Pro-rated at 500 at bats per year, my 1,081 strikeouts would mean that for two years out of the fourteen I played, I never touched the ball.

NORM CASH,
Former Tiger first baseman

PLAY BALL

Most Lifetime Hits

	PLAYER	HITS	YEARS PLAYED
1	Pete Rose	4256	1963-1986
2	Ty Cobb	4191	1905-1928
3	Hank Aaron	3771	1954-1976
4	Stan Musial	3630	1941-1963
5	Tris Speaker	3514	1907-1928
6	Carl Yastrzemski	3419	1961-1983
7	Honus Wagner	3415	1897-1917
8	Eddie Collins	3312	1906-1930
9	Willie Mays	3283	1951-1973
10	Eddie Murray	3255	1977-1996
11	Nap Lajoie	3242	1896-1916
12	Paul Molitor	3178	1978-Present
13	George Brett	3154	1973-1993
14	Paul Waner	3152	1926-1945
15	Robin Yount	3142	1974-1993
16	Dave Winfield	3110	1973-1995
17	Rod Carew	3053	1967-1985
18	Lou Brock	3023	1961-1979
19	Al Kaline	3007	1953-1974
20	Roberto Clemente	3000	1955-1972
21	Cap Anson	2995	1871-1897
22	Sam Rice	2987	1915-1934
23	Sam Crawford	2961	1899-1917
24	Frank Robinson	2943	1956-1976
25	Willie Keeler	2932	1892-1910

PLAY BALL

Pete Rose—Thorns and All

Former President Jimmy Carter once wrote a newspaper column in support of Pete Rose, banned from major league baseball and its Hall of Fame for personal problems Rose experienced off the field. Calling for forgiveness for "Charlie Hustle," Carter noted the "[e]xtenuating circumstances: The most important are the marvelous (not just superior) achievements of Pete Rose as a player during his long career, aside from his subsequent service as a manager. No player has over-hustled more, or been more committed to the game of baseball. After breaking Ty Cobb's record, Rose went on to a total of 4,256 hits in an unequaled 3,562 games and 14,053 times at bat, for a lifetime batting average of .303. He also held 31 other major and National League records." No one can deny Pete Rose's thrilling impact on the game of baseball.

He's hitting .450. Of course, everybody is hitting .450.
Braves center fielder MARQUIS GRISSOM,
on his son D'MONTE, who is playing T-ball
at the age of four.

We used to go to the racetrack after spring training practice in my day. Four of us would chip in fifty cents each to go to the two-dollar window. Yesterday I asked a player how he did at the track. He said "my horse won." I said, "How much did it pay?" The player said, "No, coach, I didn't bet on the horse, I own it."
Yankee Coach MICKEY VERNON, 1985

PLAY BALL

"Joltin' Joe" DiMaggio

He is a modern-day American icon. An athlete with grace both on and off the field. He is one of the most popular men to ever play America's favorite pastime—Joe DiMaggio.

Joseph Paul DiMaggio was born in Martine, California, on November 25, 1914. His two brothers, Dominic and Vincent, also played major league baseball.

DiMaggio's baseball career began in 1932 with the Pacific Coast League. He played in San Francisco until 1936, when he was signed by the New York Yankees. He remained there until he retired in 1951.

DiMaggio served the Yankees as one of the best outfielders ever to play the game. Nicknamed the "Yankee Clipper" for his superb fielding ability, DiMaggio also was a great offensive player as well. He set a major league record by establishing a 56-game hitting streak in 1941, which helped earn him the nickname "Joltin' Joe."

DiMaggio played in ten World Series, and was the American League's Most Valuable Player in 1939, 1941 and 1947. In 1948, he led the league with 39 home runs and 155 runs batted in.

Joe DiMaggio ended his phenomenal baseball career with 361 home runs in 1,736 games. He was inducted into the Baseball Hall of Fame in 1955. In 1986, he received the Ellis Island Medal of Honor for his achievements on the baseball field, as well as for being a worthy role model for past, present, and future youth of America.

Marilyn and Joe

Returning from a USO tour of Korea, Marilyn Monroe told her husband, Joe DiMaggio, then retired, "Oh, Joe, it was wonderful. You never heard such cheers."

"Yes, I have," was DiMaggio's clipped reply.

PLAY BALL

Triple Crown Hitters

Leading their league in batting average, home runs, and runs batted in:

PLAYER	TEAM	YEAR	AVG	HR	RBI
Paul Hines	PRV	1878	.358	4	50
Hugh Duffy	BOS	1894	.438	18	145
Nap Lajoie	PHI	1901	.422	14	125
Ty Cobb	DET	1909	.377	9	115
Heinie Zimmerman	CHC	1912	.372	14	103
Rogers Hornsby	STL	1922	.401	42	152
Rogers Hornsby	STL	1925	.403	39	143
Jimmie Foxx	PHI	1933	.356	48	163
Lou Gehrig	NYY	1934	.363	49	165
Joe Medwick	STL	1937	.374	31	154
Ted Williams	BOS	1942	.356	36	137
Ted Williams	BOS	1947	.343	32	114
Mickey Mantle	NYY	1956	.353	52	130
Frank Robinson	BAL	1966	.316	49	122
Carl Yastrzemski	BOS	1967	.326	44	121

When I was a small boy in Kansas, a friend of mine and I went fishing. I told him I wanted to be a real major league baseball player, a genuine professional like Honus Wagner. My friend said that he'd like to be President of the United States. Neither of us got our wish.

DWIGHT D. EISENHOWER,
34th President of the United States

PLAY BALL

Roberto Clemente—Superstar Gentleman

Defensively, Roberto Clemente is probably the best right fielder to ever play the game. On a base hit to right field, Roberto was always a threat to gun down a runner trying to take an extra base.

But the Pirates' number 21 was also an offensive giant, towering over his contemporaries at the plate. Consider these career highlights:

- Led the National League in batting four times ('61-.351, '64-.339, '65-.329, '67-.357)
- 3,000 career hits
- .317 career batting average
- Led the National League in hits twice ('64-211, '67-209)
- Collected over 200 hits in a season four times
- Batted .300 thirteen times during his career
- Led NL outfielders in assists five times
- 1966 National League MVP
- 1971 World Series MVP
- Inducted into the Baseball Hall of Fame in 1973
- Uniform Number 21 retired by the Pirates

Perhaps Clemente is best remembered for his humanitarian deeds. Roberto always had time to help out those less fortunate than he, especially in his homeland of Puerto Rico. In fact, he lost his life on a mission to help the people of earthquake-ravaged Nicaragua on December 31, 1972, only three months after finishing the 1972 season with his 3,000th career hit.

PLAY BALL

How to Play Pepper

The most important point to remember when learning how to hit is *"just meet the ball."* Don't swing for the fences. I have always believed that you can teach someone to be a good hitter if he is meeting the ball. But you can't teach the boy who continues to swing hard and miss all the time. When first leaning how to hit, it does not matter where or how you hit the ball, so long as you are meeting it. If you just foul the ball off, it's a step in the right direction. However, never, never take your eye off the ball. Watch it all the time. Don't look where you expect it to go because it will never get there.

Have someone pitch to you and just practice meeting the ball. The best practice routine for this is a Pepper game. Three or four boys stand abreast about twenty-five or thirty feet away from the batter. One boy throws the ball to the batter who hits it back to another fielder who in turn repeats the action. The ball is thrown slowly, because the object is to hit every ball and practice placing it accurately to each fielder. The usual procedure is to hit the ball back to the fielders on the ground. Assume your normal batting stance when hitting. If ever you miss the ball during this exercise, you can be certain that you have taken your eye off the ball.

We set the table, but no one ate.
Rangers manager JOHNNY OATES,
after his team left
14 runners on base in an
8-3 loss to Oakland.

from SPORTS spectrum

Rick Aguilera

A Man on the Run

For a pitcher, Rick Aguilera does a lot of running.

He runs from one practice field to another like a rookie trying to latch on to the team. He runs from one drill to the next as the Minnesota Twins work out.

Then he stops. A writer would like a word with him. Politely, Aguilera promises to meet him after practice.

And off he goes. Running.

He stops again. This time a young family standing by a fence has waved him over. Aguilera stops, chats, and patiently signs a few autographs.

Again, he takes off. Running.

Funny thing is, Rick Aguilera has no reason to run. He's not the kind of player with a bad past to run from. He's not the kind of player who has to hustle his feet sore to prove he's got what it takes. He's established his position in the baseball world, yet on he runs.

While he may be the one running, the thirty-six-year-old relief pitcher is the kind of person everybody in baseball ought to be running to. There ought be a long line of people trying to catch him and ask him how he can handle life and baseball with such class.

In an era when sports stars are noted for their strutting and primping and chest-thumping, Rick Aguilera is as different from that as a Roger Clemens fastball is from a Tim Wakefield knuckler.

Quiet and serious, the bearded one has developed what might be called the quintessential leadership style among major leaguers.

"I don't have to worry about him," says the Twins' tough-guy manager Tom Kelly. "He conducts himself in a classy manner. He's a professional in every way, and he's dedicated to his job."

When he stops running long enough to talk, Aguilera says of his leadership style, "I'm not a real vocal person. If there's one way I lead best, it would be by my example. Just trying to show a great work ethic and being prepared."

Aguilera's penchant for preparation has helped him put together a widely respected career as a pitcher. In thirteen years on the mound for the New York Mets, the Twins, and the Boston Red Sox, the San Gabriel, California native has appeared in 549 games and has pitched more than 1,100 innings. His 237 saves going into the '97 season put him in the top ten among active relief pitchers. He has appeared in fifteen postseason games and three All-Star contests.

As one of the game's elder statesmen, Aggie could put his career on cruise control and take it easy during the final year of his contract. For Aguilera, though, that's not possible. It'd be worse than asking him to sit out a practice session.

"We've been given this opportunity to play this game, and I think it's something players should appreciate," says Aguilera. "It's easy to take this for granted because of the attention and the salaries we get. But once you start to let that happen, it's a terrible thing. If you appreciate the blessing of the game, the least you can do is prepare yourself the best you possibly can, mentally and physically."

While some of his teammates are watching Aggie in an effort to become better players, some are following him to become better people. With those players, he has a special bond, for he is the team chapel leader for the Twins. In that role, he works with team chaplain Tom Lamphere to develop spiritual growth among his teammates. Understanding the delicate situation of supporting chapel on a team whose management has a history of being opposed to Christian athletes, Aguilera reacts characteristically to the challenge. "If I can treat the situation professionally and be faithful while respecting the organization's wishes, it will work. I don't want the guys in chapel to be late for batting practice or clubhouse meetings.

"We've had a steady growth in our chapel program, and it's been wonderful to see God's work here."

Baseball chapel played a key role in Aguilera's coming to faith in Christ. In 1985, when Aguilera was a rookie with the Mets, he met Clint Hurdle, another young Met. "He was a tremendous witness, and he really helped me to learn about having a relationship with Jesus Christ," says Aguilera. But it wasn't until three years later that Aguilera turned his life over to Jesus Christ wholeheartedly.

"I was trying to live my life on my terms. I hit a bad streak in my career, and I was wondering where I was headed. I said, 'Lord, I don't know where my life is going. You can have it. Help me to follow You wholeheartedly and put You first.' It was truly a rededication to the Lord."

Now, ten years later, Aguilera represents all that's good about both baseball and Christians in baseball. His goals as the Twins' chapel leader are clear: "Let's be concerned about one another. Let's try to meet each other's needs. Let's try to be accountable to one another. Let's try to set an example in the clubhouse for the nonbelievers in there. Let's stand tall in our faith. Let's be examples of Jesus. Let's try to show the way by the way we go about our daily work and our daily lives."

Twins second baseman Todd Walker is one of those young Christians who is learning by watching Aggie in action. "It's good to know you can always go to him and tell him what's on your mind and ask him anything. He's able to give you a straight answer. As Christians, we're supposed to be slow to speak and quick to listen. That's how Rick is."

Rick Aguilera is a man on the run. With so much to do, so many people to lead, it's a wonder he doesn't wear track shoes.

[Before that,] I couldn't drive home Miss Daisy.
Boston outfielder LEE TINSLEY,
on his first three RBI

I have no clue what any of this means. For all I know, we don't even have signs.
Angels reliever TROY PERCIVAL,
who didn't understand any of third
base coach RICK BURLESON'S signs when asked
to go to the plate for his first career at bat

The Hurlers

The Prototype Relief Pitcher

One of the relatively unsung mainstays of the '27 Yankees was an unformidable, balding Oklahoma farmer named Wilcy Moore, whom Ed Barrow had signed after reading in *The Sporting News* that he had won thirty games in the Sally League in 1926. Moore said he was twenty-eight, but he was clearly older. He had just one pitch, a sinking fastball, but he made it work through great control and, as Frank Graham wrote, "nerves of steel—or no nerves at all." Moore used to beg his manager to let him throw his curve, but the manager said to him, "Your curve ball wouldn't go around a button on my vest." Still, Moore became the prototype of the modern relief pitcher, winning 19 and saving 15 of the 50 games in which he appeared.

Moore was also a dreadful hitter, and Babe Ruth put up three hundred dollars to Moore's one hundred dollars that he wouldn't get three hits all season. Moore ended up with six hits, including a home run, and Ruth made good on his bet. After the season, Moore wrote to his benefactor: "The three hundred dollars came in handy. I used it to buy a fine pair of mules. I named one Babe and the other Ruth."

With those who don't care about baseball, I can only sympathize. I do not resent them. I am even willing to concede that many of them are physically clean, good to their mothers, and in favor of world peace. But while the game is on, I can't think of anything to say to them.

ART HILL

PLAY BALL

War Takes Mathewson

They didn't call it World War I in 1918, because it was thought to be "the war to end all wars," and hence, no Roman numeral was needed. Instead, it was "The Great War," or just "The World War." Baseball felt little of its effect in 1917, despite falling attendance, but in 1918 the players themselves were called to military service. Although President Woodrow Wilson recommended that sports continue as usual, the provost marshal issued a "work or fight" order on May 23, 1918, requiring all men of draft age either to enter military service or to obtain war-related jobs. War Secretary Newton Baker gave baseball a "grace period" that would allow the season to run through Labor Day, but it did not prevent the players themselves from taking up arms and heading for Europe, or at least into war-related jobs.

Among the 227 players who found themselves wearing military uniforms were the great pitchers Grover Cleveland Alexander and Christy Mathewson. Mathewson became one of the game's great war tragedies. Hit with poison gas during a training exercise, Captain Mathewson would develop tuberculosis and eventually die from it in 1925 at the age of forty-seven. Matty's Giant teammate, Eddie Grant, was killed in action.

I was a nervous wreck out there. I felt like I was in the presence of the president.

Mariners reserve catcher JOHN MARZANO, after hitting a double and winding up standing next to Baltimore's CAL RIPKEN JR.

Triple Crown Pitchers

Leading their league in wins, strikeouts, and earned run average:

PLAYER	TEAM	YEAR	W/L	SO	ERA
Tommy Bond	BOS	1877	40-17	170	2.11
Old Hoss Radbourn	PRV	1884	59-12	441	1.38
Tim Keefe	NYG	1888	35-12	333	1.74
John Clarkson	BOS	1889	49-19	284	2.73
Amos Rusie	NYG	1894	36-13	195	2.78
Cy Young	BOS	1901	33-10	158	1.62
Rube Waddell	PHI	1905	26-11	287	1.48
Christy Mathewson	NYG	1905	31-8	206	1.27
Christy Mathewson	NYG	1908	37-11	259	1.43
Walter Johnson	WAS	1913	36-7	303	1.09
Grover Alexander	PHI	1915	31-10	241	1.22
Grover Alexander	PHI	1916	33-12	167	1.55
Grover Alexander	PHI	1917	30-13	201	1.86
Hippo Vaughn	CHC	1918	22-10	148	1.74
Walter Johnson	WAS	1918	23-13	162	1.27
Grover Alexander	CHC	1920	27-14	173	1.91
Dazzy Vance	BRK	1924	28-6	262	2.16
Walter Johnson	WAS	1924	23-7	158	2.72
Lefty Grove	PHI	1930	28-5	209	2.54
Lefty Grove	PHI	1931	31-4	175	2.06
Lefty Gomez	NYY	1934	26-5	158	2.33
Lefty Gomez	NYY	1937	21-11	194	2.33
Bucky Walters	CIN	1939	27-11	137	2.29

PLAY BALL

PLAYER	TEAM	YEAR	W/L	SO	ERA
Hal Newhouser	DET	1945	25-9	212	1.81
Sandy Koufax	LA	1963	25-5	306	1.88
Sandy Koufax	LA	1965	26-8	382	2.04
Sandy Koufax	LA	1966	27-9	317	1.73
Steve Carlton	PHI	1972	27-10	310	1.97
Dwight Gooden	NYM	1985	24-4	268	1.53
Roger Clemens	TOR	1997	21-7	292	2.05

The two most important things in life are good friends and a strong bullpen.

BOB LEMON,
Former Cleveland pitcher

I was never nervous when I had the ball, but when I let it go I was scared to death.

LEFTY GOMEZ,
Yankee Hall of Fame pitcher

No one can stop a home run. No one can understand what it really is, unless you have felt it in your own hands and body. As the ball makes its high, long arc beyond the playing field, the diamond and the stands suddenly belong to one man. In that brief, brief time, you are free of all demands and complications.

SADAHARU OH,
Tokyo Giants outfielder
and all-time home run leader

PLAY BALL

The Rarity of Pitching Perfection

In baseball's modern history (starting in 1901) pitchers have thrown around 200 no-hit games. If at first blush this sounds like a lot, consider that the total represents the modest average of two-and-one-third no-hitters per season. Or, of the 125,000-plus games played in the majors in those seasons, only about 200 of them were no-hitters. Just about one no-hitter for every 625 games. If no-hitters are most exceptional, perfect games are almost non-existent. History records only thirteen examples of such astonishing perfection since 1901—an average of about one every eight years, or one in 11,350 games. The most recent is the perfect game thrown by David Wells of the New York Yankees, against Minnesota on May 17, 1998.

A Pitcher Pouts

Readying for his start against the St. Louis Browns, Philadelphia Athletics ace Rube Waddell tossed his last warm-up pitch. The St. Louis first base coach began his game chatter. "Get out of here you big bum," the coach hollered. "You can't pitch."

Waddell glanced over with a wounded expression, dropped his glove on the mound, walked to the outfield, and climbed into the bleachers, where he took a seat among the shirtsleeved crowd. Despite arguments and pleas from his manager and teammates, he stayed there all afternoon.

PLAY BALL

The Hop of the Fast Ball

The fastball may be the key baseball pitch; surely it is the most dramatic. How fast can a pitcher throw a ball? It seems that the fastest pitchers can throw the ball so that it crosses the plate with a velocity of about 100 mph.

Since the ball slows down considerably on the way from the pitcher to the plate, the "muzzle velocity" of the ball—as it leaves the pitcher's hand—is about eight miles per hour greater than its speed across the plate. The ball loses speed at the rate of about one mile an hour every seven feet.

It is well-known that the backspin applied to the overhand fastball causes the ball to rise—or hop; such a ball will be thrown with a backspin of perhaps 1200 rpm and rotate about eight times on its way from pitcher to plate. Though the hop is not likely to be much greater than four inches, this is more than enough to trouble the batter swinging a 2.75-inch-diameter bat because he must initiate his swing when the ball is about halfway to the plate and the deviation from the hop is only about one inch.

I'm tired of it. I don't want to hear about it anymore.
Red Sox first baseman BILL BUCKNER,
on the World Series grounder that
rolled between his legs, allowing the
New York Mets to rally to victory

The only people I ever felt intimidated by in my whole life were Bob Gibson and my Daddy.
DUSTY BAKER,
Outfielder for the Braves, Dodgers, Giants, and A's

Charles Johnson

We Pray A Lot

Charles Johnson made his major league debut on May 6, 1994, against Philadelphia. He hit a home run in his second major league at bat against Curt Schilling, and was the first player from the Marlins minor league system to make it to the majors.

In 1995 he led National League catchers in caught-stealing percentage (41.4%; 36 of 87); set a major league single-season record with 123 consecutive errorless games in 1997; set a major league career record for consecutive errorless games (172) between June 23, 1996, and March 31, 1998; and set a career record for most consecutive total chances without an error (1,295). He was traded to Los Angeles in May, 1998.

Here Johnson tells of his faith in Jesus Christ:

Q: When you made the decision to follow Jesus Christ as your Savior and Lord, what led to that life-changing event?

A: My life really changed a few years ago when my grandfather passed away. It altered my thoughts on life. I always had a knowledge of Christ, but my faith didn't come alive until that point—I said a prayer that day asking Christ to come into my life. That same year I became the chapel leader for our team.

As a young kid, I grew up in a church. I was always attending church. I was baptized and everything. But when I started to put more time in His Word, I began to truly understand and trust what God says.

I'm a young Christian, but I've really started to understand that I can do everything through Christ. I've been reading His Word and trying to live by His Word. My hope is that my faith and my beliefs will continue to draw me closer to God.

Q: You mentioned that Bible reading has helped you grow in your faith. Are there other things that have been instrumental in your spiritual growth?

A: My wife has been very helpful. She grew up studying the Word of God. And friends around me, some people on the team, have faith in Christ.

At times, being a young Christian, you can get caught up in worldly things. You think you can do it all by yourself. At times I think I can do it all by myself. So everyday I've just got to keep praying that God will help me [rely on Him].

Q: How do you and your wife, Rhonda, encourage each other in your faith?

A: We pray a lot. Before we go to bed we say a prayer together. Before we come to the field. . .throughout the day. It helps keep our faith and marriage together.

Q: What have you learned about God this season?

A: I read different psalms in the Bible, and I really enjoy Philippians 4:13, knowing that everything can be done through Christ. I pick out different verses in the Bible, different psalms, and different passages to try and keep me going.

During the course of a season there are so many more "downs" in this game than there are "ups." We fail more in baseball than we succeed. If you get three hits out of ten, you're doing very good. But that's a lot of times to fail—seven times.

It's been very difficult for me to keep going by myself. Now I can't imagine going through a season by myself without praying to God and having Him in my life.

I knew June was Pedro [Guerrero]'s favorite month, so I told him that in the U.S., June had sixty days. I'd see him in July and say, "Well, Pedro, it's June 52 and I see you're still hot."

Dodgers Manager TOMMY LASORDA,
after Pedro Guerrero hit 15 home
runs in June and .460 in July

I don't get upset over things I can't control, because if I can't control them there's no use getting upset. And I don't get upset over the things I can control, because if I can control them there's no use in getting upset.

MICKEY RIVERS,
Outfielder/DH for the Angels,
Yankees, and Rangers

Around the Horn

The Suicide Squeeze

A *squeeze play* occurs only when there is a runner on third base. As soon as the pitcher starts his delivery toward the plate, the runner breaks for home at top speed. It is the batter's job to bunt the ball far enough away from the catcher to allow the runner to score safely. It is called a squeeze play, or a suicide squeeze, because if the batter misses the ball, the runner will most likely be tagged out.

"The Base Stealer,"
by Robert Francis

Poised between going on and back, pulled
 Both ways taut like a tightrope-walker,
Fingertips pointing the opposites,
 Now bouncing tiptoe like a dropped ball
Or a kid skipping rope, come on, come on,
 Running a scattering of steps sidewise,
How he teeters, skitters, tingles, teases,
 Taunts them, hovers like an ecstatic bird,
He's flirting, crowd him, crowd him,
 Delicate, delicate, delicate, delicate—now!

Baseball is a lot like life. The line drives are caught, the squibbers go for base hits. It's an unfair game.
      Former New York Met ROD KANEHL

PLAY BALL

Lifetime Leaders in Stolen Bases

	PLAYER	STEALS	YEARS PLAYED
1	Rickey Henderson	1231	1979-Present
2	Lou Brock	938	1961-1979
3	Billy Hamilton	912	1888-1901
4	Ty Cobb	891	1905-1928
5	Tim Raines	795	1979-Present
6	Vince Coleman	752	1985-1997
7	Eddie Collins	744	1906-1930
8	Arlie Latham	739	1880-1909
9	Max Carey	738	1910-1929
10	Honus Wagner	722	1897-1918
11	Joe Morgan	689	1963-1984
12	Willie Wilson	668	1976-1994
13	Tom Brown	657	1882-1898
14	Bert Campaneris	649	1964-1983
15	George Davis	616	1890-1909
16	Dummy Hoy	594	1888-1902
17	Maury Wills	586	1959-1972
18	George Van Haltren	583	1887-1903
19	Ozzie Smith	580	1978-1996
20	Hugh Duffy	574	1888-1906
21	Bid McPhee	568	1882-1899
22	Brett Butler	558	1981-1997
23	Davey Lopes	557	1972-1987
23	Otis Nixon	557	1983-Present
25	Cesar Cedeno	550	1970-1986

PLAY BALL

Tinker to Evers to Chance

The Chicago Cubs infield produced the game's first famous double-play combination—Joe Tinker at shortstop, Johnny Evers at second, and Frank Chance at first. Although statisticians have failed to prove that they were measurably better than many other double-play combinations over the years, these three were given an edge by a classic baseball poem. Written by Franklin P. Adams in 1910 and published in the New York *Evening Mail*, it goes like this:

> *These are the saddest of possible words—*
> > *Tinker to Evers to Chance.*
> *Trio of Bear Cubs and fleeter than birds—*
> > *Tinker to Evers to Chance.*
> *Thoughtlessly pricking our gonfalon bubble,*
> > *Making a Giant hit into a double,*
> *Words that are weighty with nothing but trouble—*
> > *Tinker to Evers to Chance.*

Pretty much on the basis of this poem, the three were elected to the Hall of Fame as a unit in 1946.

The last thing you want to do is go down in the history of All-Star game competition as the only injury sustained during the team picture.

CAL RIPKEN, JR.,
whose nose was broken by Chicago White Sox reliever Roberto Hernandez, who momentarily lost his balance stepping down off a riser after the AL team picture was taken

PLAY BALL

Wild Pitch or Passed Ball?

The terms *wild pitch* and *passed ball* both refer to a pitched ball that gets away from the catcher, allowing a runner to advance to the next base. The difference is in who gets blamed for the advance. A wild pitch is considered to be the pitcher's fault, and he is charged with an error on his throw. However, if the pitch is good and the ball gets away from the catcher, it is scored a passed ball, and the catcher gets the error, since he should have caught the ball that he allowed to get past him.

I took the two most expensive aspirins in history.

WALLY PIPP,
on his decision to sit out a game
with a headache—which let
Lou Gehrig into the lineup

Fans don't boo nobodies.

Hall of Famer REGGIE JACKSON,
who played for the A's, Yankees, and Angels

The greatest thrill in the world is to end the game with a home run and watch everybody else walk off the field while you're running the bases on air.

AL ROSEN,
Former Cleveland third baseman

SPORTS
spectrum

Keith
Lockhart

Breaking Through

Keith Lockhart made his major league debut with the Padres on April 5, 1994 and banged out his first major league hit on April 7 against the Braves. The next day, in his first major league start, he hit two home runs against the Marlins, but was sent back to the minors after 43 at bats. In 1995, Lockhart was a thirty-year-old rookie with the Royals. He hit .321 in 94 games and hit .500 for the Braves in the 1997 National League Championship Series (8-16).

Keith received the 1995 Joe Burke Award from the Kansas City Royals for special achievement above the expected; was named Royals Player of the Month for September 1995 (hit .362); named Royals Player of the Month for May 1996 (hit .342); and finished second in the majors with 18 pinch-hit RBI in 1997.

For Lockhart, spiritual transformation happened early in his life. While attending Oral Roberts University, Lockhart began to notice that a couple of friends had an impressive foundation in their lives. "They had stability," Keith says. What they had, he soon found out, was a personal relationship with Jesus Christ.

Lockhart didn't think he was ready for that kind of commitment, but he was ready for pro baseball. When the school year ended, he spent the summer in Billings, Montana, a Cincinnati Reds short-season Class A team, where he hit .347. The Reds moved him up a slot to Cedar Rapids that summer.

In the fall, Lockhart went back to ORU to continue his schooling. He found himself back in the land where friends spoke freely about spiritual matters.

One day while he was attending chapel with a friend named Bombie, the speaker challenged his listeners to ask the persons seated next to them if they wanted to put their faith in Christ. Bombie leaned over to the minor leaguer and said, "Do you want to accept Christ?"

To Bombie's surprise, Lockhart said yes. The two prayed, and Lockhart asked Jesus to be his Savior.

There were times last year when people looked at the scoreboard and thought my batting average was the temperature.

Former catcher BUCK MARTINEZ,
who played for Kansas City,
Milwaukee, and Toronto

The only reason I don't like playing in the World Series is I can't watch myself play.

REGGIE JACKSON

Baseball Characters, Part One

They couldn't possibly have played anything else

Watch a troupe of basketball players loping through an airport sometime and you'll think you've died and woken up in Flamingo Park; turn them into football players and the scene becomes a convention of nightclub bouncers. . . . Ballplayers, alone among Big Three athletes, come in regular Earth-sizes that the rest of us can identify with and dream along with. . . . The legendary John McGraw, on whom even movie baseball managers are based, and wouldn't look at a pitcher under five feet, ten inches said, "Pitchers are not ballplayers," and, "Ball players are not athletes." . . . Old photographs would seem to bear out both propositions. Scrawny, bowlegged, potbellied—no physique was too bizarre for some of the old-timers, Ruth included. It seems as if the only way one could tell they were ballplayers at all was that they couldn't possibly have played anything else.

Not true at all. Vaseline is manufactured right here in the United States.

DON SUTTON,
about the rumors that he used
a foreign substance on the ball

The ball is smaller, the planets are in line, the hole in the ozone layer is bigger, and so is Juan Gonzalez.

Cubs pitcher TERRY MULHOLLAND,
on why more home runs are being hit these days

Play Ball

Uecker Speaks

Anybody with ability can play in the big leagues. But to be able to trick people year in and year out the way I did, I think that was a much greater feat.

In 1962 I was named Minor League Player of the Year. It was my second season in the Bigs.

I signed with the Milwaukee Braves for three thousand dollars. That bothered my dad at the time because he didn't have that kind of dough. But he eventually scraped it up.

I had slumps that lasted into the winter.

When I came up to bat with three men on and two outs in the ninth, I looked in the other team's dugout and they were already in street clothes.

I hit a grand slam off Ron Herbel and when his manager, Herman Franks, came out to get him, he was bringing Herbel's suitcase.

Getting to Know Bob Uecker...

Bob recently completed his twenty-fifth year as the voice of the Milwaukee Brewers. In many ways he has become the biggest star of the team.

Uecker grew up in Milwaukee and played minor league ball in many towns including Eau Claire, Wisconsin. Bob broke in with the Braves in 1962. But Uecker never made a name for himself in the big leagues. He played with the St. Louis Cardinals and Philadelphia Phillies as well as the Braves. Over his career, Bob managed a mighty .200 career batting average.

Bob earned fame for his humor, which consists mainly of deprecating his own playing ability. He made several appearances on the "Tonight Show" with Johnny Carson. In fact, Bob was such a popular guest of Carson's he made eighty appearances before Carson retired.

In 1970, Brewers owner Allan H. (Bud) Selig, a friend of Uecker's, wanted Bob to work for the organization, and in 1971 Uecker did join the team.

Initially Bob provided only a little color commentary with Brewers announcers Merle Harmon and Tom Collins. But one day the two left Uecker alone in the booth to do the play-by-play all by himself. After that baptism by fire a legend was born.

The experience of broadcasting Brewers games paid off for Uecker. ABC Sports hired Uecker to cover such events as Monday Night Baseball, the League Championship Series and World Series. Recently Uecker was hired by NBC to cover games with Bob Costas on the Baseball Network.

Although not yet enshrined in Cooperstown, Uecker has received numerous accolades. He was introduced into the Wisconsin Performing Artists Hall of Fame in 1993, and elected to the Wisconsin Broadcasters Hall of Fame in 1994.

Bob is on the Web at:

http://207.40.196.4/milwaukeebrewers/uecker.html

PLAY BALL

Yogi-isms

Lawrence "Yogi" Berra (born 1925) played for and managed both the New York Yankees and New York Mets. He was elected to baseball's Hall of Fame in 1972, but is perhaps best known for his humorous misstatements. Here are a few:

Baseball is ninety percent mental. The other half is physical.

In baseball, you don't know nothing.

I think Little League is wonderful. It keeps the kids out of the house.

It gets late early out there.

He hits from both sides of the plate. He's amphibious.

If the people don't want to come out to the park, nobody's going to stop them.

Think! How are you gonna think and hit at the same time?

The other teams could make trouble for us if they win.

If I had my career to play over, one thing I'd do differently is swing more. Those 1,200 walks I got. . .nobody remembers them.

PEE WEE REESE,
Brooklyn/Los Angeles Dodger shortstop

from **SPORTS** spectrum

Bob Patterson

Job Security

It's taken Bob Patterson of the Chicago Cubs fifteen years to find some security in major league baseball. Now he's not sure he likes it.

As a durable and successful left-handed reliever pitching in a baseball world that craves southpaws—you'd think Bob would have no trouble landing a lengthy contract. Not a multi-year million dollar job, just a solid deal that included more than one year. Think again.

When the well-traveled veteran closed out the 1997 campaign with the Cubs, it marked the first time in his career that he knew what uniform he'd be wearing the following spring.

"I don't know that it's that good," Patterson says of baseball security. "I think sometimes you need to be on that edge and rely on other things a little more. Maybe you'll work a little harder in the off-season, maybe you'll get into the Word more—so I don't know that it's such a good thing to have that stability."

Patterson can talk about his frequent lack of baseball

security without fear because he has eternal security through his faith in Jesus Christ.

"In 1985, I gave my life to Christ. Rather than worrying about another player or about finding another team, I have the faith that should one door close another will open," says Patterson. "It [faith in Christ] gives confidence." No false security there.

The difference between the old ballplayer and the new ballplayer is the jersey. The old ballplayer cared about the name on the front. The new ballplayer cares about the name on the back.

STEVE GARVEY,
Former Dodger and Padre infielder

I'm beginning to see Brooks [Robinson] in my sleep. If I dropped a paper plate, he'd pick it up on one hop and throw me out at first.

SPARKY ANDERSON,
Former Reds and Tigers manager

When I get the record, all it will make me is the player with the most hits. I'm also the player with the most at bats and the most outs. I never said I was a greater player than Cobb.

Former Red PETE ROSE,
All-time hit leader

Baseball Characters, Part Two

Casey Stengel Speaks

Charles "Casey" Stengel (1891-1975) played and managed in professional baseball from 1910 to 1965. He was inducted in the Hall of Fame in 1966, and, like Yogi Berra, is known for his quotable comments. Here are some examples:

They have shown me ways to lose I never knew existed.
> CASEY STENGEL on his 1962 Mets

The only thing worse than a Mets game is a Mets double-header.
> CASEY STENGEL on his 1962 Mets

Nobody knows this [yet], but one of us has just been traded to Kansas City.
> CASEY STENGEL to outfielder Bob Cerv

I broke in with four hits and the writers promptly declared they had seen the new Ty Cobb. It took me only a few days to correct that impression.

All right, everybody line up alphabetically according to your height.

The secret of managing is to keep the guys who hate you away from the guys who are undecided.

I couldn't have done it without my players.
> CASEY STENGEL on winning the 1958 World Series

Play Ball

Coleman Says It All

San Diego Padres broadcaster Jerry Coleman may be the modern-day Yogi Berra or Casey Stengel. Check out these verbal bloopers:

I've made a couple of mistakes I'd like to do over.

If Pete Rose brings the Reds in first, they ought to bronze him and put him in cement.

It's a base hit on the error by Roberts.

They throw Winfield out at second, but he's safe.

Johnny Grubb slides into second with a standup double.

Edwards missed getting Stearns at third base by an eyeball.

All the Padres need is a flyball in the air.

Davis fouls out to third in fair territory.

That's the fourth extra base hit for the Padres—two doubles and a triple.

Houston has its largest crowd of the night here this evening.

Montreal leads Atlanta by three, 5-1.

The first pitch to Tucker Ashford is grounded into left field. No, wait a minute. It's ball one. Low and outside.

PLAY BALL

Harry Caray. . .

. . .the beloved, long-time announcer for the Chicago Cubs, passed away recently. Here is what some folks had to say about him:

Rob Neyer (Minneapolis-St. Paul) *Star Tribune*: "Though nearly everyone will mourn Harry Caray's passing, more than a few fans won't be sorry that he's missing from the broadcast booth this spring. Harry couldn't see real well, he mangled any name of two or more syllables, and he was a shameless shill for whichever local car dealership (or whatever) ponied up the bucks. But Harry was generally honest, a rare quality compared to his younger colleagues. When the right fielder missed the cutoff man, Harry wasn't afraid to tell you even if the right fielder happened to be a Cub. And when he said, 'You can't beat fun at the old ballpark' you always felt like he meant it. I'll miss him, and from now until the day I die, I'll always think of Harry Caray during the seventh-inning stretch. *Lemme hear ya. . .*"

Stan Musial: "We're going to miss old Harry. He was always the life of the party, the life of baseball."

Steve Stone: "Harry was the most unique broadcaster I've heard in this business. His talent was not scripted or learned in any broadcasting school. . . . He was a smart man with a wonderful sense of humor who wore his heart on his sleeve. He was the fans' broadcaster."

PLAY BALL

Jack Buck: "They sent me a tape of him and said, 'We want you to be like him.' But there was no way I could do that. There's only one guy who could broadcast like him."

Terry Adams: "People told me that not only was I going to the big leagues, but I was going to meet Harry Caray. He was a big part of our club. He always hoped that we would win. He could be rough on us, but he always wanted us to do well."

Vin Scully: "He could be critical, contentious and bombastic, or he could be lovable and full of praise. . . . People in the bleachers, as well as the man in the box seat, knew they shared their love of baseball with a true fan."

Andy MacPhail: "Harry Caray's genuine affection and appreciation for our game and its fans, spanning a period of over fifty years, is never likely to be equaled. This is a sad day for the game of baseball."

The only way I'm going to get a Gold Glove is with a can of spray paint.

REGGIE JACKSON

I'm not out here to win a beauty contest.

KIRK GIBSON,
Former Tiger outfielder and DH

Walt Weiss

A Weiss Decision

Walt Weiss made his major league debut on July 12, 1987, for Oakland. He entered the game as a pinch-runner and was caught stealing. He was sent back to Tacoma. His first major league hit: September 26 vs. Chicago. In his first full season (1988), he hit his first home run (May 15) and his first career grand slam (July 10). He hit two home runs in one game on April 5, 1989, against Seattle. With the expansion Marlins in 1993, Weiss recorded these team firsts: first extra-base hit (triple), first RBI, first base on balls. Through 1997, he had hit just two of his 23 career home runs from the right side. Weiss was American League Rookie of the Year, 1988. He led National League shortstops with 99 double plays, 1995; finished second in the National League in walks with 98, 1995; and was rated best fielding shortstop by Stats, Inc., 1997. Weiss joined the Atlanta Braves as a free agent in late 1997.

Here is the story of how he came to put his faith in Jesus Christ.

During the off-season of 1995, Walt Weiss's wife, Terri, had it in her mind to attend a conference sponsored by Pro Athletes Outreach. Terri had attended a PAO meeting for players' wives in 1994, and she felt the 1995 conference for players and their wives would be good for Walt.

Walt didn't think so. He thought he would be out of place, so he told Terri he didn't want to go. "I was really intimidated," Walt says of the prospect of being around a bunch of Christian baseball players.

Terri would not be deterred. She signed the two of them up and then talked Walt into attending.

"It changed my life," he says of the meetings he had dreaded.

While at the conference, some of the troubling questions Weiss had about Christianity were answered. After reviewing the facts, he decided, "It was plain to me that Jesus walked here on earth, and He did what it says in the Bible. There was no reason for me not to open my life to Him."

Before he and Terri went back home to Aurora, Colorado, Walt accepted Jesus Christ as his Savior.

You spend a good piece of your life gripping a baseball and in the end it turns out that it was the other way around all the time.

JIM BOUTON,
Former Yankee pitcher

Baseball players are smarter than football players. How often do you see a baseball team penalized for too many men on the field?

JIM BOUTON

The Other Guys
(and Girls!)

The Beginnings of
the Negro Leagues

Though freedom for black Americans was an issue fought over in the Civil War, African-Americans found themselves excluded from many areas of society in the post-war years. Regrettably, baseball was no exception. In 1868, the National Association of Baseball Players created the first "color line" by barring teams that included "colored persons." But blacks still loved the game of baseball, and took matters into their own hands.

The first black professional team was the Cuban Giants in 1885, but the teams played as independent ball clubs until the first black league was organized in 1920. That year Rube Foster, the father of black baseball, founded the Negro National League. Three years later, in 1923, Ed Bolden formed the Eastern Colored League. These two leagues operated successfully for several years before they fell victim to financial difficulties. Other black major leagues also operated for a single season but were not able to continue on a sound fiscal basis.

Eventually, two new leagues were organized. A new Negro National League was formed in 1933 and the Negro American League was chartered in 1937. These two leagues thrived until the color line was broken. During their existence, the Negro Leagues played eleven World Series (1924-27, 1942-48) and created their own All-Star game (1933-48) that became the biggest black sports attraction in the country.

The Negro National League folded following the 1948 season and, although black teams continued to play for several years, they were no longer of major league caliber.

PLAY BALL

The demise of the Negro Leagues was inevitable as the younger black players were signed by the white major league franchises.

I thought I had it. I was twisting around like this. It grazed my glove, hit me on the head, and bounced over. I'll be on ESPN for about a month.

> Outfielder JOSE CANSECO,
> describing an unusual home run
> which he helped over the fence

I told [GM] Roland Hemond to go out and get me a big-name pitcher. He said, "Dave Wehrmeister's got eleven letters. Is that a big enough name for you?"

> EDDIE EICHORN,
> White Sox owner

When I covered the Yankees in the '60s, they had players like Horace Clarke, Ross Moschitto, Jake Gibbs and Dooley Womack. It was like the first-team missed the bus.

> Broadcaster JOE GARAGIOLA

All ballplayers should quit when it starts to feel as if all the baselines run uphill.

> BABE RUTH

Play Ball

A History of the All-American Girl's
Professional Baseball League

During World War II, chewing-gum magnate Philip Wrigley had an idea: With so many American men (including big league ballplayers) serving in the armed forces overseas, why not start a baseball league featuring women players? His idea eventually grew into the All-American Girl's Professional Baseball League.

Wrigley believed that famous managers, such as Hall of Fame players Dave Bancroft, Max Carey, and Jimmie Foxx, would draw fans to the new league. Talent for the league was abundant and it was soon evident that the women's high caliber of play was going to be the main drawing card for the fans.

In 1943 when the league began, the girls were actually playing fast-pitch softball using an underhand pitching delivery but with certain variations to make the game faster. As the league grew in the number of teams and fan support into the postwar years, fast-pitch softball rules were modified. For example, the diameter of the ball was decreased in increments from the original twelve-inch ball in 1943 to ten and three-eighths inches in 1949 and finally to nine inches, regulation baseball size, in 1954, the league's final season. Combined with overhand pitching, which also began in 1948, the smaller and livelier ball led to an increase in batting averages during the last half of the league's existence.

The AAGPBL peaked in attendance during the 1948 season, when ten teams attracted 910,000 paid fans. However, attendance declined in the following years. The All-American Girl's Professional Baseball League operated from 1943 to 1954 and represents one of the most unique periods in baseball history.

from

SPORTS
spectrum

Jason
Layne

The Light of the Lugnuts

Jason Layne is Exhibit A in the debate over why minor league baseball attendance is way up while major league attendance has leveled off.

A 24-year-old first baseman for the Wilmington Blue Rocks of the Carolina League, Jason got a phone call from a friend, telling him to pick up a copy of *Baseball Weekly*. When he got his copy and opened the paper, Layne saw a familiar face inside. His.

"There was a picture of me standing there. It was the beginning of a short story about how his 1997 team, the Lansing Lugnuts, captured the Midwest League title. My friend was amazed with what she saw, as I was."

Unjaded by big dollars and gaudy success, Layne is sincerely thrilled by such an occurrence in his life. "God has been so good to me in all avenues of my life, especially baseball," says the six foot, three inch Texan. "There are people throughout the baseball world that never win one championship. I've had the opportunity to be a part of two championships [the Southwest Conference title in college and the 1997 Lugnuts' win]. Granted, it was college baseball and minor league baseball, but a championship is a championship."

Layne put his faith in Jesus Christ while attending junior college in his hometown of Tyler, Texas. "My coach was instrumental in introducing me to God and His Son, Jesus! It was the best decision ever to trust Christ!"

Now the hard-working, hard-hitting Layne is trying to move up the baseball ladder—battling his own perfectionistic tendencies and benefiting by his desire to please God in every aspect of his life. "I use my faith every day. My faith in God helps me cope with the temptations every minor leaguer has. Any tough situation I'm in, I look for God's way out."

Jason is the kind of guy you hope gets in the express lane from Wilmington to Kansas City.

I've had so many x-rays that my pitches might take on a subtle glow. It will be tough to pick up my ball. It will look like an opaque-type fog.

JOE MAGRANE,
Former Cardinal pitcher

Just because I'm left-handed and quotable doesn't mean I'm from another solar system.

JOE MAGRANE

The majority of American males put themselves to sleep by striking out the batting order of the New York Yankees.
Author JAMES THURBER

The Homers

How He Became "The Babe"

He was George Ruth when the first train ride of his life brought him to Fayetteville, North Carolina, in March 1914. When he left a month later, he was Babe Ruth, or simply The Babe, and that is how he would be known from then on, even in places where few people had ever heard of baseball.

He was the butt of horseplay and practical jokes and the kind of razzing all young rookies endured in those days. But Baltimore Orioles owner Jack Dunn had promised to keep a protective eye on him, and apparently he kept that promise. One day, a coach cautioned the veterans about George Ruth: "You'd better be careful," said the coach. "He's one of Dunn's babes." Ruth was the baby, or babe, of the training camp after that.

When I was a little boy, I wanted to be a baseball player and join the circus. With the Yankees, I've accomplished both.

GRAIG NETTLES,
Former Yankee third baseman

Who cares how long they are as long as they're over the fence.

White Sox third baseman ROBIN VENTURA,
on a tape-measure homer

PLAY BALL

Who is Hank Aaron?

Henry Louis "Hank" Aaron, born in Mobile, Alabama, February 5, 1934, is American baseball's all-time champion home run hitter. Aaron entered the record books on April 8, 1974, by breaking Babe Ruth's record of 714, and he went on to hit a total of 755 homers before completing his twenty-three-year major league career.

Aaron began playing professionally for all-black teams in Mobile, Alabama, and Indianapolis, Indiana, but he signed with the National League's Milwaukee Braves organization at the age of eighteen. He reached the major leagues when he was only twenty and quickly established himself as one of the game's finest players. He played for the Braves almost exclusively, first in Milwaukee (1954-65), then in Atlanta (1966-74). He ended his career with the American League's Milwaukee Brewers (1975-76). Along with a lifetime batting average of .305, Aaron had 2,297 runs batted in (first all-time), 6,856 total bases (first), 12,364 at bats (second), 3,771 hits (third), 3,298 games played (third), and 624 doubles (eighth). Aaron was the NL's Most Valuable Player in 1957, and the right fielder won three Gold Glove awards for his fielding prowess. He led the NL in home runs, runs batted in, and slugging average four times each, and in batting average twice (1956: .328; 1959: .355). In a poll of about a half-million fans in the summer of 1989, Aaron's 715th career home run was voted "the greatest moment in baseball history."

Winning is better than the next worse thing.

BILL LEE,
Former Red Sox and Expos pitcher

Play Ball

All-time Home Run Leaders

	PLAYER	HOME RUNS	YEARS PLAYED
1	Hank Aaron	755	1954-1976
2	Babe Ruth	714	1914-1935
3	Willie Mays	660	1951-1973
4	Frank Robinson	586	1956-1976
5	Harmon Killebrew	573	1954-1975
6	Reggie Jackson	563	1967-1987
7	Mike Schmidt	548	1972-1989
8	Mickey Mantle	536	1951-1969
9	Jimmie Foxx	534	1925-1945
10	Ted Williams	521	1939-1960
10	Willie McCovey	521	1959-1980
12	Ernie Banks	512	1953-1971
12	Eddie Mathews	512	1952-1968
14	Mel Ott	511	1926-1947
15	Eddie Murray	504	1977-1996
16	Lou Gehrig	493	1923-1939
17	Willie Stargell	475	1962-1982
17	Stan Musial	475	1941-1963
19	Dave Winfield	465	1973-1995
20	Mark McGwire	457	1986-Present
21	Carl Yastrzemski	452	1961-1983
22	Dave Kingman	442	1971-1986
23	Andre Dawson	438	1976-1996
24	Billy Williams	426	1959-1976
25	Darrell Evans	414	1969-1989

PLAY BALL

Four-Homer Games

The following are the twelve players who have hit four home runs in a single game:

NATIONAL LEAGUE

PLAYER	TEAM	DATE
Bobby Lowe	Boston	May 30, 1894
Ed Delahanty	Philadelphia	July 13, 1896
Chuck Klein	Philadelphia	July 10, 1936
Gil Hodges	Brooklyn	August 31, 1950
Joe Adcock	Milwaukee	July 31, 1954
Willie Mays	San Francisco	April 30, 1961
Mike Schmidt	Philadelphia	April 17, 1976
Bob Horner	Atlanta	July 6, 1986
Mark Whiten	St. Louis	September 7, 1993

AMERICAN LEAGUE

PLAYER	TEAM	DATE
Lou Gehrig	New York	June 3, 1932
Pat Seerey	Chicago	July 18, 1948
Rocky Colavito	Cleveland	June 10, 1959

I don't want to play golf. When I hit a ball, I want someone else to go chase it.

ROGERS HORNSBY

Play Ball

The 1998 Home Run Chase

Mike Eisenbath of the St. Louis *Post-Dispatch* wrote on
Monday, September 28, 1998:

> Mark McGwire brought a tall tale to life Sunday
> afternoon at Busch Stadium.
>
> He hit his 70th home run.
>
> Go ahead. Laugh. Laugh the giddy laugh of disbe-
> lief, of absurdity, of sheer joy. Men, whether they are
> named Babe Ruth or Roger Maris or Roy Hobbs, don't
> hit 70 home runs in one baseball season. It didn't make
> sense until Sunday, when the big, redheaded first base-
> man in a Cardinals uniform swatted two home runs on a
> day that made sense only in cheap novels, bad movies,
> and this most wonderful of baseball seasons.

McGwire and Sosa

Baseball fans will never forget the 1998 season, a campaign which included the New York Yankees' record-setting 114 victories and unprecedented twenty-fourth World
Series championship. But what really sets 1998 apart is
that incredible home run chase—the daily slug-fest between "Big Mac" Mark McGwire and "Slammin' Sammy"
Sosa. They battled to see not just *whether* Roger Maris's
thirty-seven-year-old record of 61 home runs in a season
would fall, but by *how many*. Both did indeed surpass
Maris—Sosa finished the year with an incredible 66
homers, and McGwire reached the rarified air of *70*. Making their chase all the more wonderful, though, was Mark
and Sammy's terrific sportsmanship throughout. Each cred-
ited the other with pushing him to greater accomplishments,

and who can forget their embrace when McGwire's Cardinals played Sosa's Cubs late in the season? Just who are these guys who almost single-handedly restored baseball to its former popularity as "America's Pastime"?

Here is how they look in a reference book:

Mark McGwire
Born: October 1, 1963, Pomona, CA
Baseball 1B

Sporting News college player of the year (1984); Member of 1984 U.S. Olympic baseball team; won AL Rookie of the Year and hit rookie-record 49 HRs in 1987; broke Roger Maris's season home run record (61) 1998 with St. Louis; only player with at least 50 HRs in three straight seasons.

Sammy Sosa
Born: November 12, 1968, San Pedro de Macoris,
   Dominican Republic
Baseball OF

Born into an impoverished family in Dominican Republic; played first major league game in 1989 with the Texas Rangers; joined Mark McGwire in memorable chase of Roger Maris's single-season home run record, finishing with 66 (second most ever); hit 102 homers in two seasons to surpass Cubs' record of 95 set by Hack Wilson in 1929-30.

PLAY BALL

Giving back

In a time when professional athletes are known more for their selfishness than their generosity, McGwire and Sosa have again broken from the pack. Both are giving back to society, through the Mark McGwire Foundation for Children (helping youngsters suffering from abuse), and the Sammy Sosa Foundation (an organization raising funds for underprivileged children in the Chicago area and the Dominican Republic). For his efforts on and off the field, McGwire has earned the "*Sporting News* Sportsman of the Year Award," and Sosa was named a recipient of the Gene Autry Courage Award, honoring athletes who have demonstrated heroism or overcome hardships to inspire others.

The Rumble

In case you missed any of Mark McGwire's or Sammy Sosa's home runs, here is a complete breakdown of their record-setting 1998 season:

MARK MCGWIRE

HR Number	Date	vs. Pitcher
1	3/31	Ramon Martinez (LA)
2	4/2	Frank Lankford (LA)
3	4/3	Mark Langston (SD)
4	4/4	Don Wengert (SD)
5	4/14	Jeff Suppan (Ariz)
6	4/14	Jeff Suppan (Ariz)

HR Number	Date	vs. Pitcher
7	4/14	Barry Manuel (Ariz)
8	4/17	Matt Whiteside (Phil)
9	4/21	Trey Moore (Mon)
10	4/25	Jerry Spradlin (Phil)
11	4/30	Marc Pisciotta (ChC)
12	5/1	Rod Beck (ChC)
13	5/8	Rick Reed (NYM)
14	5/12	Paul Wagner (Mil)
15	5/14	Kevin Millwood (Atl)
16	5/16	Livan Hernandez (Fla)
17	5/18	Jesus Sanchez (Fla)
18	5/19	Tyler Green (Phil)
19	5/19	Tyler Green (Phil)
20	5/19	Wayne Gomes (Phil)
21	5/22	Mark Gardner (SF)
22	5/23	Rich Rodriguez (SF)
23	5/23	John Johnstone (SF)
24	5/24	Robb Nen (SF)
25	5/25	John Thomson (Col)
26	5/29	Dan Miceli (SD)
27	5/30	Andy Ashby (SD)
28	6/5	Orel Hershiser (SF)
29	6/8	Jason Bere (ChW)
30	6/10	Jim Parque (ChW)
31	6/12	Andy Benes (Ariz)
32	6/17	Jose Lima (Hou)
33	6/18	Shane Reynolds (Hou)

Play Ball

HR Number	Date	vs. Pitcher
34	6/24	Jaret Wright (Cle)
35	6/25	Dave Burba (Cle)
36	6/27	Mike Trombley (Min)
37	6/30	Glendon Rusch (KC)
38	7/11	Billy Wagner (Hou)
39	7/12	Sean Bergman (Hou)
40	7/12	Scott Elarton (Hou)
41	7/17	Brian Bohanon (LA)
42	7/17	Antonio Osuna (LA)
43	7/20	Brian Boehringer (SD)
44	7/26	John Thomson (Col)
45	7/28	Mike Myers (Mil)
46	8/8	Mark Clark (ChC)
47	8/11	Bobby Jones (NYM)
48	8/19	Matt Karchner (ChC)
49	8/19	Terry Mulholland (ChC)
50	8/20	Rick Reed (NYM)
51	8/20	Willie Blair (NYM)
52	8/22	Francisco Cordova (Pit)
53	8/23	Ricardo Rincon (Pit)
54	8/26	Justin Speier (Fla)
55	8/30	Dennis Martinez (Atl)
56	9/1	Livan Hernandez (Fla)
57	9/1	Donn Pall (Fla)
58	9/2	Brian Edmondson (Fla)
59	9/2	Robby Stanifer (Fla)
60	9/5	Dennis Reyes (Cin)

PLAY BALL

HR Number	Date	vs. Pitcher
61	9/7	Mike Morgan (ChC)
62	9/8	Steve Trachsel (ChC)
63	9/15	Jason Christiansen (Pit)
64	9/18	Rafael Roque (Mil)
65	9/20	Scott Karl (Mil)
66	9/25	Shayne Bennett (Mon)
67	9/26	Dustin Hermanson (Mon)
68	9/26	Kirk Bullinger (Mon)
69	9/27	Mike Thurman (Mon)
70	9/27	Carl Pavano (Mon)

SAMMY SOSA

HR Number	Date	vs. Pitcher
1	4/4	Marc Valdes (Mon)
2	4/11	Anthony Telford (Mon)
3	4/15	Dennis Cook (NYM)
4	4/23	Dan Miceli (SD)
5	4/24	Ismael Valdes (LA)
6	4/27	Joey Hamilton (SD)
7	5/3	Cliff Politte (StL)
8	5/16	Scott Sullivan (Cin)
9	5/22	Greg Maddux (Atl)
10	5/25	Kevin Millwood (Atl)
11	5/25	Mike Cather (Atl)
12	5/27	Darrin Winston (Phil)
13	5/27	Wayne Gomes (Phil)

PLAY BALL

HR Number	Date	vs. Pitcher
14	6/1	Ryan Dempster (Fla)
15	6/1	Oscar Henriquez (Fla)
16	6/3	Livan Hernandez (Fla)
17	6/5	Jim Parque (ChW)
18	6/6	Carlos Castillo (ChW)
19	6/7	James Baldwin (ChW)
20	6/8	LaTroy Hawkins (Min)
21	6/13	Mark Portugal (Phil)
22	6/15	Cal Eldred (Mil)
23	6/15	Cal Eldred (Mil)
24	6/15	Cal Eldred (Mil)
25	6/17	Bronswell Patrick (Mil)
26	6/19	Carlton Loewer (Phil)
27	6/19	Carlton Loewer (Phil)
28	6/20	Matt Beech (Phil)
29	6/20	Toby Borland (Phil)
30	6/21	Tyler Green (Phil)
31	6/24	Seth Greisinger (Det)
32	6/25	Brian Moehler (Det)
33	6/30	Alan Embree (Ariz)
34	7/9	Jeff Juden (Mil)
35	7/10	Scott Karl (Mil)
36	7/17	Kirt Ojala (Fla)
37	7/22	Miguel Batista (Mon)
38	7/26	Rick Reed (NYM)
39	7/27	Willie Blair (Ariz)
40	7/27	Alan Embree (Ariz)

Play Ball

HR Number	Date	vs. Pitcher
41	7/28	Bob Wolcott (Ariz)
42	7/31	Jamey Wright (Col)
43	8/5	Andy Benes (Ariz)
44	8/8	Rich Croushore (StL)
45	8/10	Russ Ortiz (SF)
46	8/10	Chris Brock (SF)
47	8/16	Sean Bergman (Hou)
48	8/19	Kent Bottenfield (StL)
49	8/21	Orel Hershiser (SF)
50	8/23	Jose Lima (Hou)
51	8/23	Jose Lima (Hou)
52	8/26	Brett Tomko (Cin)
53	8/28	John Thomson (Col)
54	8/30	Darryl Kile (Col)
55	8/31	Brett Tomko (Cin)
56	9/2	Jason Bere (Cin)
57	9/4	Jason Schmidt (Pit)
58	9/5	Sean Lawrence (Pit)
59	9/11	Bill Pulsipher (Mil)
60	9/12	Valerio De Los Santos (Mil)
61	9/13	Bronswell Patrick (Mil)
62	9/13	Eric Plunk (Mil)
63	9/16	Brian Boehringer (SD)
64	9/23	Rafael Roque (Mil)
65	9/23	Rodney Henderson (Mil)
66	9/25	Jose Lima (Hou)

from **SPORTS** spectrum

A Fearless Faith

The 1998 New York Yankees

Members of the 1998 World Champion New York Yankees tell of their fellowship and faith:

Q. What are some factors in this team's success?

Chad Curtis: One of the main things is confidence, and confidence is such a major part of baseball. We've jelled together as a team to where we not only have confidence in ourselves, but we have confidence in each other. We have such a large group of guys who are unified through something that's much larger than baseball. We hold that as more important.

Q: Not only are you a great baseball team, but you also have a strong Christian presence. What led to this phenomenon on the Yankees?

Andy Pettitte: This year has been a great year! Chad had the idea of getting together and having devotions every day before batting practice. We have Bible studies on the road. There's nothing better for Christian brothers than to fellowship together. You know you're talking with someone who really cares about what's going on in your life.

Chad: It's something the Lord laid on my heart early—it's a truth from His Word. Wherever two or more are assembled, the body of Christ is present. So many times when there's a group of Christians you focus on the things that are different, and it splinters the group. What we've been able to do through the power of Christ and His Word is to unify ourselves by the common bond we have and not focus on the things that would divide us and play into the enemy's hands. We focus on how we're like-minded, and how to move forward as one body so we can do the work He has set before us.

Q: What spiritual activities do you do on a regular basis to remain strong?

Darren Holmes: Chad has a group of tapes from Focus on the Family that takes us back to Jerusalem and the Promised Land. They take us into places where Jesus did His ministry and where things happened in the New Testament and in the Old Testament. We usually get together and do that the second day in every city. About twenty minutes before stretching, we read a devotional and take prayer requests and pray. And it's not just one guy, we have the whole group. Sometimes people feel out of place praying aloud in front of other guys, but everybody in here is looking toward the same goal. That's what's unique—there's no shyness. When you're sitting on the bench, there's fellowship there. When I'm in the bullpen—there's fellowship there. It seems that God has placed us and dispersed us throughout this team. From the coaching staff, to the people who work in the clubhouse, to those in the bullpen, to the starting staff, to the relievers, to the regular players—it's amazing how we've all mixed in and unified and lifted one another up.

Chad: One thing that's unique about our fellowship is that we have not sequestered ourselves into a group and said, "This is us and that is them." We've tried to be intentional about ministering to those who aren't in the group right now. It's exciting that we're doing this interview today because last night we had two guys in our group who had the opportunity to witness to a third guy, and he received the Lord last night. The names aren't as important as the fact that a soul is entered into eternity! We're not looking at God as some type of good-luck charm. We're trying to fulfill the commission that He's put before us—to teach and to preach and to make disciples. We've seen proof of that this year since some of the guys have accepted the Lord. That's where the real glory is!

Q: Is there any resistance to the spiritual atmosphere on this team?

Andy: I don't think so. There's such a large group of guys on this team that it's not really an issue.

Joe Girardi: Some people might think that because God is in control we don't look at the wins and losses. And because we look at how to serve the Lord that we might be weak as players. You can ask people— we go out and play for Jesus Christ, so we have a responsibility to Him and to our teammates to give it everything we have. We play the game with an enormous amount of intensity.

Chad: The guys on our team who are not a part of our group see the authenticity of our group. They realize that there's nothing to belittle. I think the guys who aren't a part of our group have no choice but to respect the players who are a Christian influence on this team because of the group's effort to keep the walk.

Q: Chad, your name is often mentioned as the leader of the Christians on this team. In what ways has your spiritual journey made it possible for you to be in such a position?

Chad: It's kind of a tough issue because I know the Bible says that a leader will be held more accountable than someone who is not a leader. It's probably something I try to avoid. But when God puts you in a position to be able to do His work, then you need to accept that. There have been times when I chose to serve baseball or chose to serve my next contract, and God has shown me that's fruitless. He's worked it out in my life to allow me to have a more eternal perspective and more of a desire to do His work. I've been tested through fire, and God has refined me. It hasn't always been a pleasant process, but I know that it was for my good. I continue to fail, and He continues to lift me up. He continues to work on me. I just thank God for the opportunity He's given me to fellowship with the guys on this team.

Q: How has your faith helped you play in a "glass house" that is legendary throughout sports— Yankee Stadium?

PLAY BALL

Scott Brosius: It's been a great source of strength and encouragement. When you have a group of guys like this who get together on a daily basis and stay in the Word—you stay fresh. I learned a lesson last year in Oakland, where I went through a really difficult year. As I was going through that, the same people who had been on my bandwagon were the ones who were ready to boot me out of town. It was a good lesson to understand that while men will change, God never changes. There's no greater confidence than knowing that God is in control of your life.

Andy: It gives me great peace to know that no matter how good or how bad I do, the Lord loves me. That's all that really matters to me. Baseball isn't what everything is about. It's about the way I'm being a Christian husband, a Christian father, or the way I'm living my life and trying to be a Christian testimony to people.

Q: Let's look at the flip side of the success of this team. If you were 35 games out of first place, how would the spiritual atmosphere on this team change?

Darren: I came from the Rockies. My first year, we won something like 65 games. I didn't feel like spiritually it was any different than what I'm experiencing here. We had a good spiritual mix on that team. When we were going bad, we still had fellowship. I didn't notice a difference in my spirituality.

Joe: I think our perspective is always the same. Our perspective is to live godly lives. Do our best for the Lord Jesus and spread His gospel. Wins and losses will not change what our perspective is in life. I've been on good teams and I've been on bad teams, but our perspective is still the same. We go out there every day and do our best to glorify Jesus. Whether we win or we lose is not in our control. So our perspective isn't going to change. Whether we're 30 games over .500 or 50 below, it will always be the same.

Scott: This is the one thing that is mentioned a hundred times throughout the year: We don't use God as a good-luck charm. We're not getting together because we think He's giving us wins! The character and confidence this team has is a result of the Christian influence and the core group of guys. It certainly wouldn't change anything in this group if we were 35 games out.

Chad: One of our phrases that we use; "God is not our good-luck charm, He's a life-giver." Which would you rather have? Would you rather be given eternal life through His Son, or be given good luck while you're walking the face of the earth? That's where the perspective comes in. We're more thankful to Him for what He's done for us here as a group than we are for the wins and losses. We are thankful for those wins and losses, but that's not our main concern. Giving God the glory is not a matter of who won a game. Giving God the glory is giving Him the glory because He is God. He is in control. I used to think of "giving God the glory" as when I hit a home run I've got to make sure I give Him credit. I've gotten beyond that. I realize that giving God the glory is accepting the failure in a way that still honors Him. I think last year Tony Fernandez was the perfect example of that. He had a game-winning home run against Baltimore that put his team into the World Series. When they were interviewing him he said, "Hey, I give God the glory for that. He's my Lord and Savior. He gives me the strength to do that." And then in the World Series, he booted a ball that cost them the whole World Series. After the game they interviewed him again, and He didn't turn around and say, "Oh well, I curse God because He didn't allow me to make the play." He said, "Jesus Christ is still my Savior and Lord, and I still honor Him. It just didn't work out the way I wanted it to." The game is not the end. The end is Christ.

Q: Scott, you're one of the newest members of this team. Were you surprised to find such a strong Christian influence with the Yankees?

Scott: One of the first nights we were here, a group of guys were sitting around talking about how they ended up with the Yankees. Everyone had the same story: "Boy, the last place I wanted to go was the Yankees," or "When I was a free agent the Yankees were the last team on my list—yet here I am!" And here you have this whole group of Christians saying the same story. It became pretty apparent that this whole thing wasn't put together by us. This whole thing was God-driven. This group is together for a reason.

Q: Are you surprised by the closeness of the Christian group on this team? And are you surprised at how God has moved among you?

Chad: God is faithful to give us fellowship. There's also an element that we have to be obedient to assemble that fellowship together. This year we decided to do that, and I think God has honored us. I think of the group of guys on our team, I could name each one, and I could tell you areas that I've personally seen growth. I've seen guys grow spiritually this year. It says in the Bible "a tree is known by its fruit." The fruit that I've seen growing out of some of the guys this year has been positive. That's a testimony to the fact that God has been working on us.

Darren: On the teams I've played on in the past you usually have one guy that's a so-called "leader." Then, you usually have quite a few guys who are followers. Chad is our leader. Chad's a very good organizer, and he really takes the steps to get things going. But every guy in this room has shown leadership qualities. That's what's unique to me. I've seen a group of guys where there's not just one leader, but there's four or five leaders.

Andy: I came up with the organization. I'm in my fourth season, and it seems like I've been here longer than any other guy on the team. Scott talked about coming to spring training and guys saying this was the last place they wanted to be. I was at the point where I didn't even want to come this year because we lost some players I had gotten close to. We lost some good Christian guys I had fellowship with. I just got aggravated. But to see how it's worked out, where Christian brothers were coming over, and we've had some guys get saved—it's just been an unbelievable blessing!

The secret of my success was clean living and fast outfielders.

LEFTY GOMEZ

Some Final Funnies

I led the league in "Go get 'em next time."

BOB UECKER

That's Hendrick's nineteenth home run. One more and he reaches double figures.

JERRY COLEMAN

You have to have a catcher because if you don't you're likely to have a lot of passed balls.

CASEY STENGEL

I set records that will never be equaled. In fact, I hope ninety percent of them don't even get printed.

BOB UECKER

Tony Taylor was one of the first acquisitions that the Phillies made when they reconstructed their team. They got him from Philadelphia.

JERRY COLEMAN

Jerry Lumpe looks like the best hitter in the world until you put him in the lineup.

CASEY STENGEL

Career highlights? I had two. I got an intentional walk from Sandy Koufax and I got out of a rundown against the Mets.

BOB UECKER

The ex-left-hander Dave Roberts will be going for Houston.

JERRY COLEMAN

PLAY BALL

Ability is the art of getting credit for all the home runs somebody else hits.

CASEY STENGEL

The way he's swinging the bat, he won't get a hit until the twentieth century.

JERRY COLEMAN

You look up and down the bench and you have to say to yourself, *Can't anybody here play this game?*

CASEY STENGEL

When I looked at the third base coach, he turned his back on me.

BOB UECKER

Mike Caldwell, the Padres' right-handed southpaw, will pitch tonight.

JERRY COLEMAN

I was such a dangerous hitter I even got intentional walks in batting practice.

CASEY STENGEL

Wait until it stops rolling and pick it up.

BOB UECKER,
on how to catch a knuckleball

Over the course of a season, a miscue will cost you more than a good play.

JERRY COLEMAN

PLAY BALL

I don't like them fellas who drive in two runs and let in three.

CASEY STENGEL

Sporting goods companies pay me not to endorse their products.

BOB UECKER

I sure hope you're staying alive for the upcoming Dodgers series.

JERRY COLEMAN

The way our luck has been lately, our fellas have been getting hurt on their days off.

CASEY STENGEL

Baseball hasn't forgotten me. I go to a lot of Old-Timers games and I haven't lost a thing. I sit in the bullpen and let people throw things at me. Just like old times.

BOB UECKER

References

Tony Fernandez: I Need Something Better in My Life—from *Sports Spectrum,* June 1998.

The Origin of Baseball—Adapted from "Why Cooperstown?" Copyright 1997 by National Baseball Hall of Fame and Museum, Inc.

The Beginning of Professional Baseball—from *Album of Baseball* by Harvey Frommer. Franklin Watts, New York. 1988.

The Baseball Shrine of Pigtown—from *Baseball, An Illustrated History* by Geoffrey C. Ward. Alfred A. Knopf, New York. 1994.

The House Built for Ruth—from *Dynasty: The New York Yankees 1949-1964* by Peter Golenbock. Prentice-Hall, New York. 1975.

Andy Benes: The Benes Factor—from *Sports Spectrum,* July/August 1998.

The Modern World Series Begins—from *The World Series, The Story of Baseball's Annual Championship* by Lee Allen. G. P. Putnam's Sons, New York. 1969.

Red Sox Win the Series!—from *Peanuts and Crackerjack* by David Cataneo. Rutledge Hill Press, Nashville. 1991.

The National League and Jackie Robinson—from *Only the Ball Was White* by Robert Peterson. Oxford University Press, New York. 1992.

Baseball Is Not Life Itself…—from *Season Ticket, A Baseball Companion* by Roger Angel. Houghton Mifflin Company, Boston. 1988.

Terry Steinbach: Catching the Rock—from *Sports Spectrum,* July/August 1998.

Cobb's Average at 52—from *Rain Delays* by Burt Randolph Sugar. St. Martin's Press, New York. 1990.

Pete Rose: Thorns and All—from "It's Time to Forgive Pete Rose" by Jimmy Carter. *USA Today,* October 30, 1995.

"Joltin' Joe" DiMaggio—from the Italian-American Web Site of New York (http://www.italian-american.com/joedimag.htm)

How to Play Pepper—from *How to Hit* by Johnny Mize. Henry Holt and Company, 1953.

Rick Aguilera: A Man on the Run—from *Sports Spectrum,* July/August 1998.

The Prototype Relief Pitcher—from *Baseball Anecdotes* by Daniel Okrent and Steve Wulf. Harper and Row, New York. 1990.

War Takes Mathewson—from *Great Moments in Baseball* by Tom Seaver with Mary Appel. Carol Publishing Group, New York. 1992.

The Rarity of Pitching Perfection—adapted from *The Ol' Ball Game.* Stackpole Books, New York. 1990.

A Pitcher Pouts—from *Peanuts and Crackerjack* by David Cataneo. Rutledge Hill Press, Nashville. 1991.

The Hop of the Fastball—from *The Physics of Baseball* by Robert Kemp Adair. Harper & Row, New York. 1990.

Charles Johnson: We Pray A Lot—from *Sports Spectrum,* July/August 1998.

The Suicide Squeeze—from *The Great Sports Question and Answer Book.* I. Waldman & Son, New York. 1979.

Tinker to Evers to Chance—adapted from *Great Moments in Baseball* by Tom Seaver with Mary Appel. Carol Publishing Group, New York. 1992.

Wild Pitch or Passed Ball?—from *The Great Sports Question and Answer Book.* I. Waldman & Son, New York. 1979.

Keith Lockhart: Breaking Though—from *Sports Spectrum,* July/August 1998.

They Couldn't Possibly Have Played Anything Else— from *Baseball and Lesser Sports* by Wilfrid Sheed. Harper Collins, New York. 1991.

Bob Patterson: Job Security—from *Sports Spectrum,* July/August 1998.

Walt Weiss: A Weiss Decision—from *Sports Spectrum*,
   July/August 1998.

The Beginnings of the Negro Leagues—adapted from
   "History of Black Baseball and the Negro Baseball
   Leagues" by James A. Riley. Copyright 1996.
   (http://www.blackbaseball.com/introd.htm)

A History of the All-American Girl's Professional
   Baseball League—adapted from "League History,
   All American Girl's Professional Baseball League
   1943-1954." Copyright 1997, 1998.
   (http://www.dlcwest.com/~smudge/history.html)

Jason Layne: The Light of the Lugnuts—from *Sports
   Spectrum*, June 1998.

How He Became "The Babe"—from *Baseball
   Legends—Babe Ruth* by Norman L. Macht. Chelsea
   House Publishers, Philadelphia. 1991.

Who Is Hank Aaron?—from *I Had a Hammer: The
   Hank Aaron Story* by Henry Aaron and Lonnie
   Wheeler. Harper Mass Market, New York. 1991.

A Fearless Faith—the 1998 New York Yankees—from
   Sports Spectrum, October 1998 (with Kevin
   Hunter). Kevin Hunter is a sportswriter who lives
   in Long Beach, California.

LIKE JOKES OR TRIVIA?

Then check out these great books from
Barbour Publishing!

*A Funny Thing Happened on My Way through
the Bible* by Brad Densmore
 A different twist on the traditional Bible
trivia book. Share it with family and friends!
 Paperback. $2.49

*500 Clean Jokes and Humorous Stories and
How to Tell Them* by Rusty Wright and Linda
Raney Wright
 Everything you need to improve your
"humor quotient"—all from a Christian
perspective.
 Paperback. $2.49

Fun Facts about the Bible by Robyn Martins
 Challenging and intriguing Bible trivia—
expect some of the answers to surprise you!
 Paperback. $2.49
